Knots & Splices

Jeff Toghill

FERNHURST BOOKS

Published in Great Britain by
Fernhurst Books
13 Fernhurst Road London SW6 7JN

First published by
A H & A W REED PTY LTD
2 Aquatic Drive Frenchs Forest NSW 2086 Australia
68 Kingsford-Smith Street Wellington 3 NZ

First published 1979
Reprinted 1980, 1981, 1982, 1984

© Jeff Toghill 1979

ISBN 0 906754 11 9

Printed and bound by Everbest Printing Co Ltd, Hong Kong

CONTENTS

Know your ropes

Types of rope

Rope comes in all shapes and sizes, but is generally constructed of one of three materials—natural fibre, synthetic fibre or wire. Originally all rope was made from natural fibre, then came wire. Since World War II, the trend has been towards synthetic fibre, although wire rope is still widely used. Natural fibre ropes have gradually been displaced and are seen only rarely these days. Boats, in particular, tend to use wire and synthetic fibre ropes almost exclusively for rigging.

Natural fibre

As a general rule, these are composed of the fibres of the leaf and stem of tropical plants or grasses. They are not generally as strong as synthetic fibre ropes and are susceptible to rot when wet. Although fibre ropes such as Manila, Hemp and Sisal are still used for specific purposes, the synthetic ropes have a greater strength and longer life and are thus more widely used.

Synthetic fibre

Four principal synthetics are used in the construction of synthetic fibre rope—Nylon, Polyester (commonly known as 'Terylene', its trade name), Polypropylene, and Polyethylene. Nylon and Polyester are the most commonly used, although the other two synthetics have properties which make them ideal for certain work. One of these properties is that, unlike the other two synthetic ropes, they float.

Wire

The two main forms of wire rope are galvanised 'plough' steel wire and stainless steel wire. Both have good properties and are used widely for all kinds of purposes. On board boats, stainless steel is more popular because it does not rust with use. Wire rope is usually in one of two categories—flexible rope which is very workable and allows the wire to be wound around the drum of a crane or winch or through pulleys in a tackle, and the stiffer, non-flexible rope which is used where no bending is required, such as the rigging of yachts and radio masts.

Strength

A good guide to the respective strengths of fibre ropes of equal size can be seen when breaking strain is compared.

Manila	4 tonnes
Polyethylene	6 tonnes
Polypropylene	7 tonnes
Polyester	8 tonnes

Stretch

All ropes stretch under load and it is important to know how much, particularly in cases such as mountaineering ropes. A rough guide to comparable stretch factors of fibre ropes is as follows.

Nylon stretches	to 45% of its length
Polypropylene	to 35% of its length
Polyethylene	to 35% of its length
Polyester	to 25% of its length
Natural fibre	to about 15% of its length

Deterioration

All ropes deteriorate with wear, and some deteriorate under the influence of weather or chemicals. Natural fibre ropes, for example, are very susceptible to rot while wire and synthetic ropes are not. However, galvanised wire can rust and synthetic ropes can be seriously affected by heat or sunlight. Chemicals such as acids attack most materials and damage from abrasion is one of the most common causes of deterioration in any ropes.

Construction

As mentioned earlier, ropes can come in all shapes and sizes, but the two most common forms of rope construction are LAID rope and BRAIDED rope. Fibre ropes may be made up either way, but wire rope is usually laid. PLAITED rope, which is similar in appearance to braided rope, is also used extensively for certain types of work.

LAID rope is the traditional 'twisted' rope usually of three separate strands wound around each other. BRAIDED and PLAITED ropes consist of an outer 'woven' sheath of yarns covering an inner core. Laid rope is stronger and less liable to stretch than the other types, but tends to be harder to handle and has a 'stiffer' feel.

Parts of a rope

The following terms are used in describing parts of a rope used for tying knots or splicing:

End	The last few centimetres of the rope.
Standing part	The main length of rope.
Bight	A curve in the rope created by bringing the end to the standing part but not crossing them.
Loop	Formed by crossing the end over the standing part.
Lay	The way in which the strands are made up or twisted to form the rope (laid rope only).
Strands	The individual layers of fibre twisted together to form the rope.
Yarns	Each individual fibre.

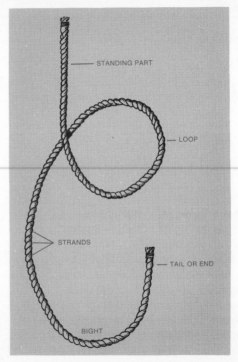

Coil	The circular method of tidying up loose rope. Some ropes coil clockwise, others anti-clockwise.
Flake	A 'zig-zag' method of laying down a rope so that it can run out freely.
Cleat	To secure the end of the rope to some object (usually a cleat).

Knots and splices

Knots and splices are used for a variety of purposes. Simple stopper knots, for example, merely prevent a rope from running through an eye or pulley. A complex long splice, by contrast, makes it possible to join two pieces of rope together in such a way that they *can* run through an eye or pulley. There are practical knots which simply join two pieces of rope together and there are fancy knots which have little practical use but make excellent decorations when worked around certain fittings such as a handrail or a boat's tiller.

Natural fibre and synthetic ropes can usually be knotted or spliced, although splicing braided or plaited rope is a fairly involved process and is not often encountered. Wire ropes, however, are rarely knotted due to the stiffness of the steel strands, and joining wire ropes invariably means splicing. This is a complex procedure and too involved to deal with in a booklet such as this, as also is the practice of joining wire to braided synthetic rope. Nowadays, most of these splices are done by machine.

Sailors' knots are so called because they are very secure when tied properly, but never jam and can be readily undone, even when the rope is wet. Boy scout's knots are the same in most cases, since even if the rope does not get wet, it can still jam when under load if an incorrect knot is used. The knots in this book all fall into the category of nonjamming knots and thus have a variety of uses both afloat and ashore.

Stopper knots

Overhand knot

Use
Preventing a rope running through a block.

Method
1 Pass the end of the rope over the standing part to create a loop.
2 Take the end down over the standing part and under the loop.
3 Continue by bringing the end of the rope up through the loop.
4 Pull tight.

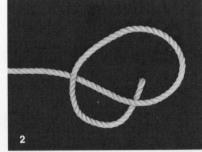

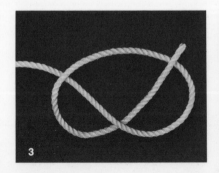

Figure of eight knot

Use

Preventing a rope running through a block. Commonly used for the sheets of a sailing boat.

Method

1 Pass the end of the rope over the standing part.
2 Take the end under the standing part away from the loop.
3 Bring the end of the rope back up over itself towards the loop.
4 Pass the end down through the loop.
5 Pull tight.

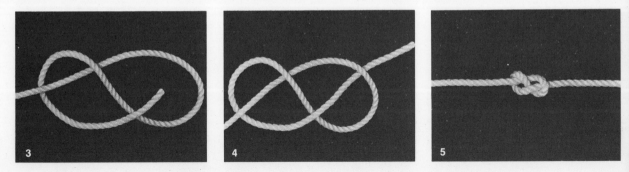

Hitches

Half hitch

Use

Widely used for securing the end of a rope, but somewhat doubtful as a single half hitch. More commonly used in the form of two half hitches.

Method

1 Pass the end of the rope through or around the object to which it is to be secured.
2 Pass the end of the rope over and around the standing part thus creating a loop.
3 Continue passing the end of the rope right round the standing part and back through the loop.

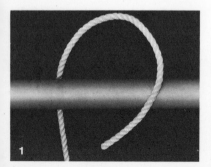

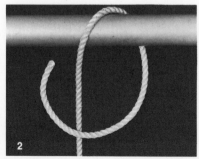

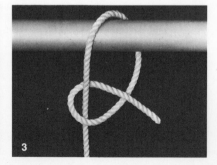

Two half hitches

Use

A more secure method of attaching the end of a line than a single half hitch.

Method

1 Form one half hitch around the standing part.
2 Take the end of the rope over and around the standing part again below the first half hitch.
3 Bring the end of the rope up through the loop so formed and pull tight.

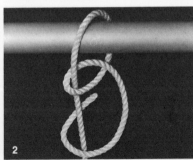
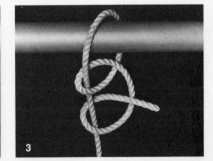

Round turn and two half hitches

Use

An excellent hitch for securing the end of a rope to any object.

Method

1 Pass the end of the rope through or around the object.
2 Pass it around again without crossing over itself.
3 Take the end of the rope over the standing part and make a half hitch.
4 Continue with the end of the rope over the standing part again and bring it up through the loop to form a second half hitch.

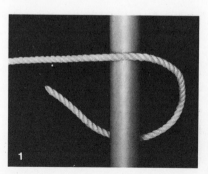

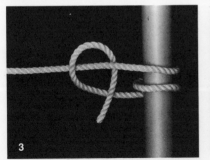

Fisherman's bend

Use

One of the most secure of all knots for attaching the end of a line to any object. Sometimes, as its name denotes, used for attaching a fishing line to a hook.

Method

1 Take the end of the rope around the object.
2 Take it around again without crossing itself, leaving the loop so formed fairly loose.

3 Take the end of the rope around the standing part as though to make a half hitch, but pass it up through the loop formed round the object.
4 Continue with the end of the rope making a second half hitch around the standing part of the rope.

Clove hitch

Use

For securing a rope to a railing or similar object.

Method

1 Pass the end of the rope over the railing and back round crossing over its own standing part.
2 Continue by passing the end over the railing again thus creating a loop.
3 Pass the end right round the railing.
4 Bring the end back through the loop so formed.
5 Pull tight.

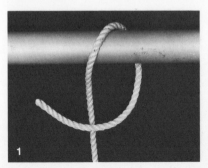

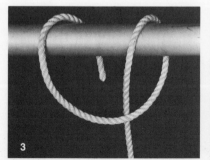

Rolling hitch

Use

For securing a line to a railing or another rope where the strain is expected to be parallel or nearly parallel to the line of the railing or other rope. It creates a form of 'jam' hitch but can be easily released.

Method

1 Pass the end of the rope over the railing or other rope and around and back over its own standing part.
2 Take another turn around the railing without crossing over any part of the knot.

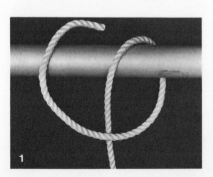

3 Take yet another turn around the railing without crossing any other part of the knot. At this point it is easy to see where the knot derives its name.
4 Pass the end of the rope under the last two turns or 'rolls' of the rope around the railing and pull tight.

NOTE When using this method, the strain must be placed on the end of the rope and not on the standing part.

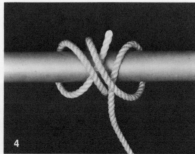

Rolling hitch (alternative method)

Use
As before, but this time the strain can be placed on the standing part rather than the end of the rope.

Method
1 Pass the end of the rope round the railing or other rope and over its own standing part.
2 Pass the end of the rope around the railing again crossing the standing part as before.
3 Pass the end of the rope around the railing and back through its own loop as with a clove hitch.

Chinese hitch

Use

Used for the same purposes as a clove hitch, but makes a more secure fastening. This hitch is, in effect, a clove hitch with one or more half hitches on the standing part.

Method

1 Form a clove hitch around the rail.
2 With the end of the rope make a half hitch around the standing part. Two half hitches make for even greater security.

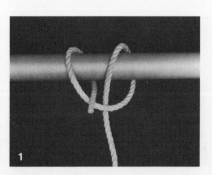

Timber hitch

Use
A very secure hitch to pass round a log or wide railing.

Method
1 Pass the end of the rope around the railing.
2 Pass the end of the rope over the standing part and back through
   the loop to form a half hitch.
3 Twist the rope over itself and back under and through the loop.
4 Repeat this as many times as necessary to jam the hitch securely.
5 Pull tight.

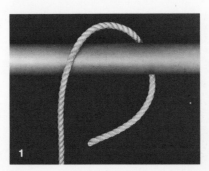

NOTE Although this hitch looks well and truly jammed, it will free easily when the strain is taken off the standing part.

Bends

Single sheet bend

Use

For joining together two pieces of rope. Of particular use when the two pieces of rope are of different sizes.

Method

1 Create a bight in the end of one rope.
2 Pass the end of the second rope up through the bight and over the end of the first rope.
3 Continue the end of the second rope round behind the end and standing part of the first rope so that it completely encircles the bight.

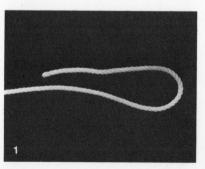

4 Pass the end of the second rope under its own standing part to form, in effect, a half hitch around the bight.
5 (alternative method) By taking the end of the second rope around the bight of the first rope in the opposite direction, a similar hitch will be obtained but one which is generally considered less likely to slip.

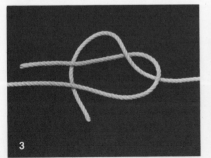

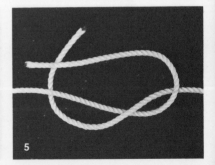

Double sheet bend

Use

A stronger hitch than a single sheet bend when joining ropes of unequal size.

Method

1 Begin as for a single sheet bend, bringing the end of the second rope up through and around the bight of the first rope.
2 Take the end of the second rope under its own standing part to make the single sheet bend, but instead of stopping at this point take the end back round the bight again.

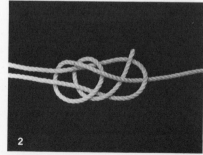

3 Finish the hitch as before by passing the end of the second rope
   under its own standing part.

NOTE The alternative method for tying a single sheet bend can also
be used for the double sheet bend.

Reef knot

Use

For joining together two ropes of equal size.

Method

NOTE There are a number of methods of tying a reef knot and many 'old salts' would not agree with the method offered here. However, without doubt this is the simplest system and other methods can be adopted later when you have familiarised yourself with the knot.

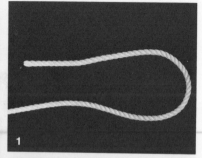

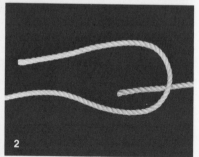

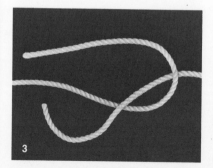

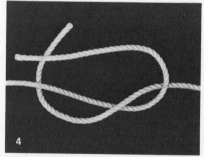

1 Form a bight in the first rope.
2 Bring the end of the second rope up through this bight.
3 Take the end of the second rope over the standing part of the first.
4 Pass the end of the second rope round behind the standing part
  and the end of the first rope thus completely encircling the bight.
5 Bring the end of the second rope back over the end of the first
  rope.
6 Pass the end of the second rope down through the bight alongside
  its own standing part.
7 Pull tight.

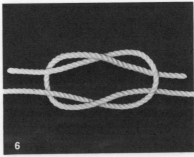

Carrick bend

Use

One of the strongest bends which will not jam. Frequently used for large size ropes.

Method

1 Form a loop in the first rope with the end over the standing part.
2 Bring the end of the second rope behind but *not* through the loop.
3 Pass the end of the second rope up over the end of the first rope.
4 Continue by passing the end of the second rope behind the standing part of the first rope and back towards the loop.

5 Pass the end of the second rope across the loop of the first rope, passing under its own standing part.
6 Pull tight.

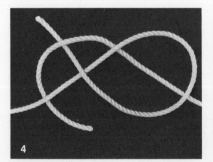

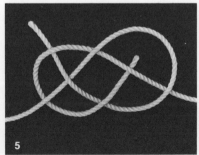

Fisherman's knot

Use

For joining together two ropes of similar size. A very strong knot often used by fishermen to join their lines, hence the name.

Method

1 Place the end of the two ropes together allowing an overlap of about 0.5 metre (depending on the size of the rope).
2 Take the end of the first rope over and under the second rope and under its own standing part to form a loop.

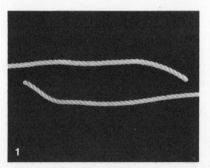

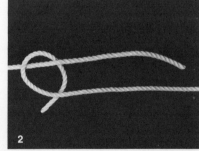

3 Take the end of the first rope up and through this loop to make an overhand knot in the end of the first rope, around the standing part of the second.
4 Repeat the process with the end of the second rope making an overhand knot around the standing part of the first rope.
5 Pull tight. The two overhand knots will slide together to jam as a secure bend.

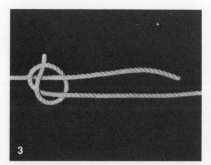

Loops

Bowline

Use
To form a loop which will not slip, but unties easily.

Method
1 Measure off the size of the loop required and create a small loop in the standing part of the rope by passing the end *over* the standing part.
2 Bring the end of the rope up through the small loop and around the back of the standing part.
3 Continue by passing the end of the rope back down through the small loop.
4 Pull tight.

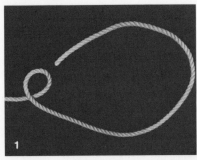

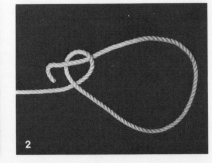

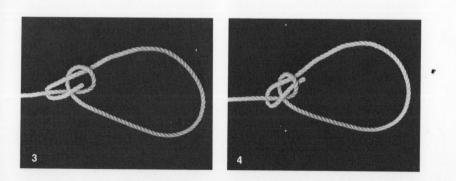

Bowline on the bight

Use

For making a double loop or sling. Often used for hoisting a man aloft or unloading barrels or other long objects.

Method

1 Form a bight by doubling the rope. The bight now, in effect, becomes the end of the rope. Form a small loop on the standing part in the same way as for a normal bowline.
2 Pass the bight up through this loop as for a normal bowline knot.

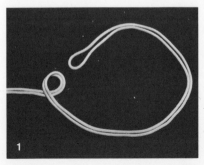
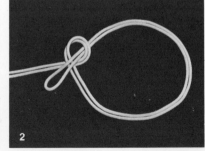

3 Pull the bight through until the large loop is the required size.
Open the bight and pass it right round the large loop.
4 Tighten up the bight so that it forms a knot around the standing
part.

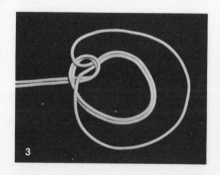

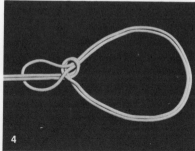

Running bowline

Use

To form a loop which is required to slip and tighten.

Method

1 Create a small bowline in the end of the rope.
2 Pass the other end of the rope through the loop thus formed.
3 Draw the standing part through until the required size of loop is formed.

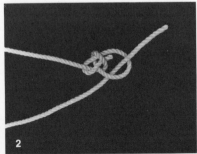
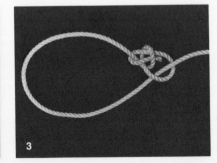

Special knots

Surgeon's Knot

Use

For joining two ends of rope. Has the advantage of holding the first tie tight while the second tie is being completed. Used in surgery.

Method

1 Place the left hand end over the right.
2 Pass the left hand end over and under the right twice, in effect twisting the left hand rope around the right.
3 Bring both ends back to meet one another.
4 Pass the left hand end (which has now in effect become the right hand end) over and under the other end. Pull tight.

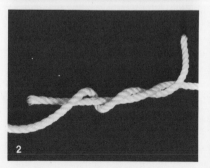

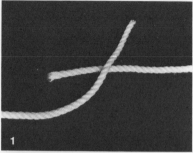

Sheepshank

Use
Shortening a rope.

Method
1 Shorten the rope to the required length by creating two bights somewhere along its length.
2 Form a small loop in one end of the rope by passing the end under the standing part.
3 Pass the bight through the loop thus formed.

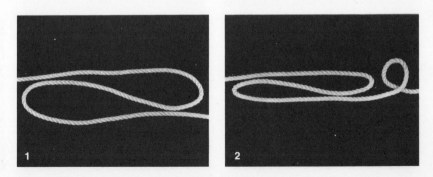

4 Form a similar loop at the other end.
5 Pass the other bight through this loop and pull tight on both standing parts.

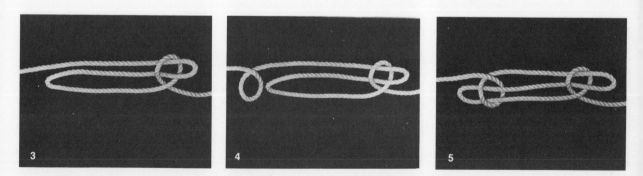

Monkey's fist

Use

Principally to form the weight at the end of a throwing line, but also widely used as a decorative or ornamental knot.

Method

1 Make three coils in the end of the rope.
2 Take the end of the rope around these three coils.
3 Make three more coils around and at right angles to the lay of the first three.
4 Take the end of the rope through the loop thus formed and around the second group of coils.

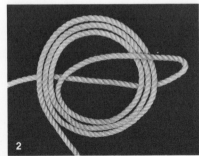

5 Make three more coils around the second group.
6 Work the knot until the coils line up in parallel, and gradually
   tighten.

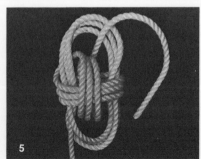

Turk's head

Use

Ornamental knot often used to decorate a tiller, make fenders, etc.

Method

1 Make a turn around the tiller or other object to be decorated without crossing the end of the rope over the standing part.
2 Pass the end round the tiller again, this time crossing over the standing part.
3 Pass the end of the rope under and through the loop formed by the last turn round the tiller.

4 Turn the knot half a turn towards you, at which point two round turns around the tiller will be revealed. Pass the left hand turn under the right hand turn.

5 Take the end of the rope over the first turn, under the second turn, and back over the first turn again.

6 Jiggle the whole knot into shape and a single turk's head will be formed.

7 By following the turns with the end of the rope a double turk's head can be made.

8 The treble turk's head, which is the most common and popular version of this knot, is made by following the turns around once more.

Wall knot

Use

As a stopper knot, or for preventing the end of a newly cut rope from unlaying.

Method

1 Unlay the rope for a few centimetres.
2 Bend the left hand strand over to form a loop.
3 Pass the middle strand behind the left hand strand and bring it up through the loop and over the end of the left hand strand, leaving a loop formed in the middle strand.

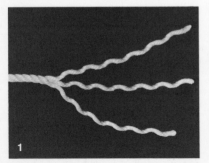

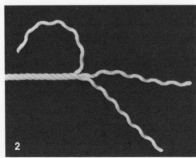

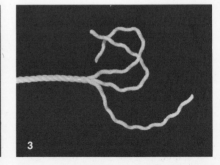

4 Pass the right hand strand in the same way behind the middle
strand and up through the loop thus formed.
5 Take the end of the left hand strand and pass it up through the
loop formed in the right hand strand. All ends of strands should
now be passing up through the loop formed in their adjacent
strand.
6 Pull tight.

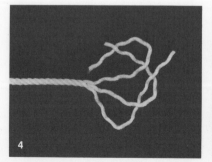

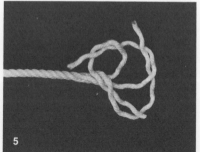

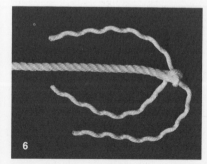

Crown knot

Use

As a stopper knot to prevent the end of rope unlaying, and as the preliminary to a back splice.

Method

1 Unlay the end of the rope for a few centimetres.
2 Form a loop in the left hand strand.
3 Pass the middle strand over the left hand strand and down through the loop.

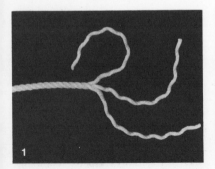
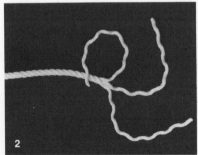
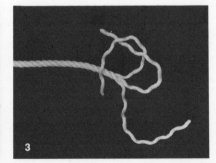

4 Repeat the procedure, passing the right hand strand over the middle strand and down through its loop.
5 Pass the left hand strand over the right and down through its loop.
6 Pull tight.

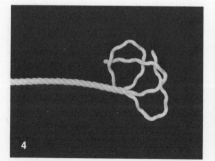

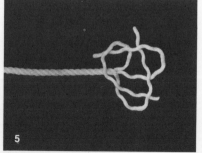

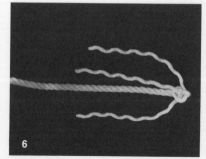

Splices

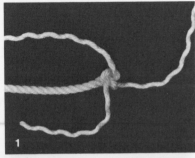

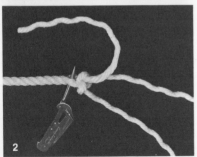

Back splice

Use

For finishing off the end of a rope and preventing it from unlaying.

Method

1 Commence with a crown knot.
2 Using a spike, loosen the first strand below the crown knot.
3 Taking the adjacent left hand strand, pass it under the loosened strand against the lay.
4 Turn the rope to the right and repeat the process with each of the other strands. Pull each strand end tight until they snug close in to the laid strands of the standing part of the rope.

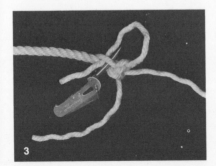

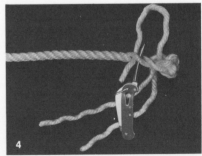

5 Continue the splice, passing each strand end over and under a strand in the laid part of the rope working always against the lay. Pull each strand end tight to snug the splice together as the work progresses.

6 When sufficient splicing has been done, taper the splice by leaving out first one then two strand ends.

7 Trim off the strand ends and roll the splice between your hands to snug the whole thing into shape.

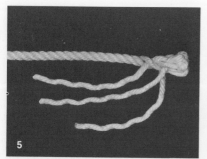

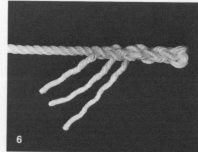

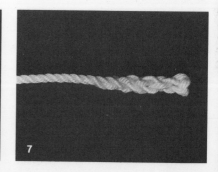

Eye splice

Use

To splice an eye or loop in the end of a rope.

Method

1 Form an eye or loop in the end of the rope to the required size and unravel the strands.
2 Using the spike, open up the standing part and thread the centre of the three unravelled strands against the lay of the rope.
3 Repeat the procedure with the next strand.
4 Turn the rope around and repeat the procedure with the third strand as illustrated.

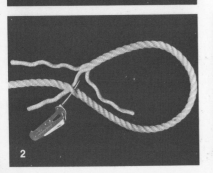

5 Pull the strands tight. Continue the splice with the same over and under tucks as used in the back splice.
6 Taper the splice as described for a back splice.
7 Trim off the ends and roll the splice to finish it.

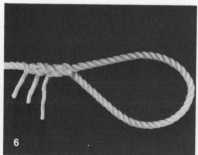

Short splice

Use

To splice two ends of rope.

Method

1 Unlay both ends of rope for a few centimetres.
2 'Marry' the unlaid ends so that the strands are alternated.
3 Secure one set of ends tightly.
4 Take any one of the unsecured strands and, using the spike, tuck it under a strand of the other rope, against the lay.
5 Repeat the procedure with all three unsecured strands.

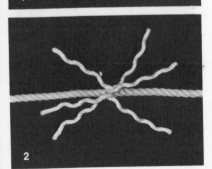

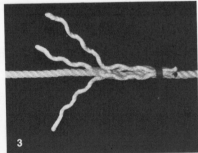

6 Continue the splice with over and under tucks and taper it as described for a back splice.
7 Repeat the procedure with the other strands working against the lay of the other rope.
8 Cut off the loose ends of the strands and roll the splice to finish it.

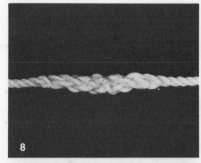

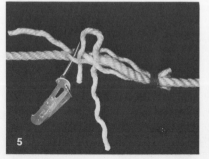

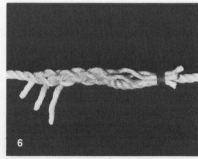

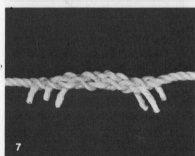

Long splice

Use
To splice together two ropes without increasing the thickness.

Method
1 Unravel the ends of both ropes for some considerable distance and 'marry' them together as described for a short splice.
2 Taking two opposing strands, unlay one backwards along the standing part following it with the opposing strand thus, in effect, relaying the rope in its original form, with the second strand.
3 Continue this procedure until there is little left of the strand being laid up.

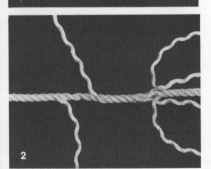

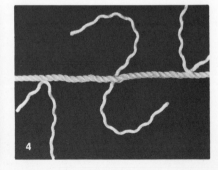

4 Repeat, working with another set of strands along the standing part of the opposite rope. Leave the remaining two opposing strands at the juncture of the splice.
5 Tie off each pair of strands with an overhand knot.
6 Work the overhand knots into the lay of the rope.
7 Unlay each strand into at least half its own diameter and tuck it away in the form of a short splice against the lay, as illustrated. The more the strand is divided, the neater the finished splice. Repeat with all strands and roll the splice to finish it.

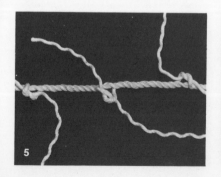
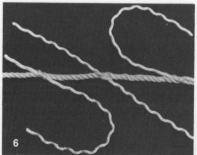
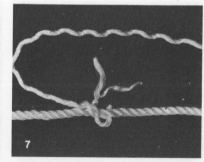

Other rope work

Whipping

Use

For preventing the end of the rope unlaying.

Method

1 Allowing sufficient whipping twine for the whole exercise, form a bight and lay it along the rope near the end to be whipped.
2 With the end of the twine passed over the standing part, commence the whipping, keeping good tension on each turn of the twine. As the whipping progresses, use your finger or a spike to ensure that the lay is even and tidy.

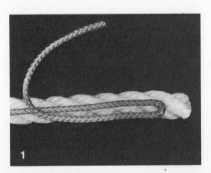 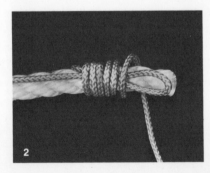

3 When sufficient whipping has been laid, pass the end of the twine through the bight formed earlier.
4 Pull the standing part of the twine tight and draw the bight under the whipping until it is completely concealed. Cut off the standing part close to the initial turn of the whipping.
5 Illustrating the location of the concealed bight of whipping twine through each stage of the procedure.

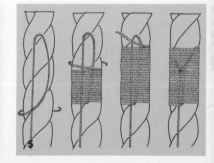

Seizing

Use

For joining together two pieces of rope without a knot or splice. Often used to form a loop or eye.

Method

1 Place the two pieces of rope to be seized close together and parallel. Place one end of the seizing twine along the ropes to be joined.
2 With the other end of the twine, commence the seizing by working the twine around the two ropes, binding them tightly together and including the first end of the seizing twine.

3 Continue until sufficient seizing has been laid, then bring the second end of twine up between the two ropes. The first end of twine should be sticking out alongside it.

4 Take the second end of twine over the top of the seizing and down between the two ropes at the other end. Continue around the seizing and back up between the ropes alongside the first end of seizing twine again. Repeat this procedure, binding the seizing tightly as you do so.

5 At the back of the seizing, join the two ends of twine tightly in a reef knot and work them into the binding.

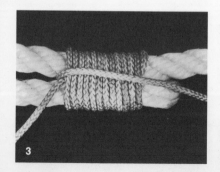

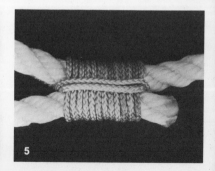